FIRST PEOPLES

THE ABORIGINAL PEOPLES

OF AUSTRALIA

ANNE BARTLETT

Lerner Publications Company • Minneapolis

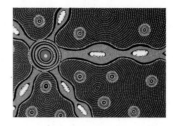

**First American edition published in 2002
by Lerner Publications Company**

Lerner Publications Company
A division of Lerner Publishing Group
241 First Avenue North
Minneapolis, MN 55401 U.S.A.
Website address: www.lernerbooks.com

Series originated and designed by
Times Editions
An imprint of Times Media Private Limited
A member of the Times Publishing Group
1 New Industrial Road, Singapore 536196
Website address: www.timesone.com.sg/te

Series editors: Margaret J. Goldstein, Karen Kwek
Series designers: Tuck Loong, Geoslyn Lim
Series picture researcher: Susan Jane Manuel

Published by arrangement with Times Editions

Library of Congress Cataloging-in-Publication Data
Bartlett, Anne.
The Aboriginal peoples of Australia / by Anne Bartlett.
p. cm. — (First peoples)
Includes bibliographical references and index.
ISBN 0-8225-4854-2 (lib. bdg. : alk. paper)
1. Australian aborigines—History—Juvenile literature.
2. Australian aborigines—Social life and customs—Juvenile
literature. 3. Torres Strait Islanders—History—Juvenile
literature. 4. Torres Strait Islanders—Social life and
customs—Juvenile literature. [1. Australian aborigines.
2. Torres Strait Islanders.] I. Title. II. Series.
GN666.B37   2002
994'.0049915—dc21   2002000331

Printed in Singapore
Bound in the United States of America

1 2 3 4 5 6—0S—07 06 05 04 03 02

CONTENTS

AUSTRALIA'S FIRST PEOPLE

Aborigine is a name for the original or earliest known inhabitants of a country or place. The word comes from the Latin term *ab origine,* which means "from the beginning." But Australia's original people, or first people, do not call themselves Aborigines. Different groups have different names, depending on which language they speak and where they live. For example, the Koori people come from Koori lands, in the modern-day states of Victoria and New South Wales, and the Murri people live in present-day Queensland. Instead of using these names, however, Europeans arriving in Australia in the late 1700s called all the original people "Aborigines."

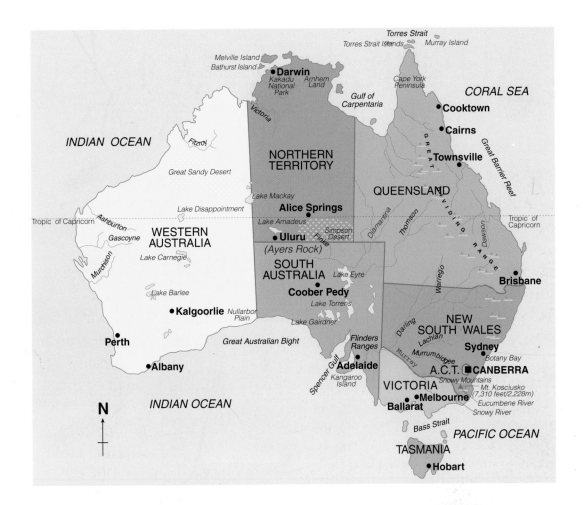

Modern First People

Australia's first people are divided into two main groups—the Aboriginal people of mainland Australia and the southern island state of Tasmania, and the Torres Strait Islanders, who live on the Torres Strait Islands, between the northeastern tip of Australia and Papua New Guinea. Modern first people number only about 265,000 and make up only about 1.6 percent of the Australian population. More than two-thirds of them live in cities, away from the homelands of their ancestors.

WHO IS ABORIGINAL?

Sometimes it's hard to tell if someone is Aboriginal or not. Aboriginal people originally had dark skin. But because many modern Aboriginal people have European as well as Aboriginal ancestors, they may have fair hair or fair skin. According to the Australian government, an Aboriginal person is someone with Aboriginal ancestors who chooses to call himself or herself an Aboriginal person. Other Aboriginal people must also recognize the person as one of them.

AUSTRALIA—A LAND OF CONTRASTS

The sixth largest country in the world, Australia covers an area of about 2,966,000 square miles (7,681,940 square kilometers)—about the size of the United States, excluding Alaska. Australia is surrounded entirely by water. The country lies in the Southern Hemisphere (the southern half of the earth). Its land is mostly flat, with only a few low mountain ranges.

Above: Parts of the Northern Territory have lush green vegetation.

Summer in December

Because Australia is located in the Southern Hemisphere, its seasons are opposite to those in the United States and other countries north of the equator. Summer in Australia lasts from December through February. Winter lasts from June through August. Summer temperatures can soar above 100 degrees Fahrenheit (37.8 degrees Celsius). Winter temperatures rarely fall below 32 degrees Fahrenheit (0 degrees Celsius) in most places, although the southeastern states sometimes have winter snow.

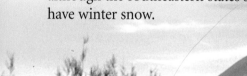

A Dry Land

Much of Australia, especially the central region, is very dry. About two-thirds of the country gets less than 15 inches (38 centimeters) of rainfall per year. But the tropical north and coastal areas receive more rainfall than the rest of the country. Parts of the Northern Territory and Queensland have tropical rain forests. Because the rest of the land is so dry, more than three-quarters of the Australian population lives near the coast, in the cities of Perth, Adelaide, Melbourne, Hobart, Canberra, Sydney, Brisbane, and Darwin. Very few people live in the dry central desert of Australia.

Above: The Simpson Desert lies in dry central Australia.

The Australian Outback

The "outback" is the name for the dry inland areas of eastern Australia and the desert regions of western and central Australia. Few people live in the outback, but Australians raise cattle and sheep on large farms called stations. "The bush" is another name for the outback and other areas far away from cities.

GIANT ROCKS

Australia's Northern Territory is known for its tors, or giant rocks. The most famous of these is Uluru (*left*)—an Aboriginal word that means "Great Pebble." Rising to a height of more than 1,000 feet (305 meters), this sandstone rock is 2.2 miles (3.5 kilometers) long and 1.5 miles (2.4 kilometers) wide. The Anangu people of the Northern Territory consider the site sacred. In 1872, white Australians named the rock after Sir Henry Ayers, a South Australian leader. For many years, it was called Ayers Rock. In 1985, the Australian government gave official ownership of Uluru and its surrounding land to the Anangu people.

UNUSUAL ANIMALS

Above:
A koala eats the leaves of the eucalyptus, or gum, tree.

Three different kinds of mammals live in Australia. Egg-laying mammals include the platypus (an animal with a bill like a duck's and shiny gray fur) and the echidna (a spiny, insect-eating animal with a long snout and long claws). Another group of mammals, marsupials, are born very tiny, before their bodies are fully developed. After birth, babies creep into their mothers' pouches and nurse there for weeks until they are fully developed and able to move around on their own. Marsupials include kangaroos, wombats, and koalas. Other Australian mammals, such as whales, dingoes (wild dogs), and bats, are born fully developed.

Right: Wallabies are members of the kangaroo family.

Kangaroos

Australia has more than forty types of kangaroos, ranging from small wallabies weighing 6 to 9 pounds (3 to 4 kilograms) to big red kangaroos weighing as much as 180 pounds (82 kilograms) and standing as tall as 6 feet (1.8 meters). Most kangaroos have small heads, small forelegs, and big powerful back legs. These back legs enable kangaroos to hop and leap at great speeds. Gray kangaroos can travel up to 30 miles (48 kilometers) per hour. Australia's first people traditionally hunted kangaroos for their meat and skins.

Lots of Reptiles

Australia is home to about 380 types of reptiles, including snakes, lizards, and crocodiles. Many of the country's snakes, including the death adder, taipan, brown snake, and tiger snake, are poisonous. The northern Australian coast is home to dangerous saltwater crocodiles, which sometimes attack people. Their harmless relatives, the smaller freshwater crocodiles, live in rivers and lakes.

Above: The saltwater crocodile can grow up to a length of 23 feet (7 meters).

The Birds of Australia

More than 600 types of birds live in Australia. One of the most well known is the emu, which stands more than 5 feet (1.5 meters) tall. Emus can't fly, although they can run at great speeds. Like ostriches, emus have small heads, long necks, and powerful legs. Common Australian birds include parrots, magpies, cockatoos, and finches.

WATER LOVERS IN THE DESERT

To survive in the hot Australian desert, some frogs absorb water through their skin, almost doubling their weight. Then they burrow about 12 inches (30 centimeters) beneath the bottom of waterholes. Their outer skins form watertight coverings around their bodies, keeping the frogs moist. They can stay buried for months through the heat of summer, even after the surface water dries up. In the dry season, thirsty Aboriginal people killed these frogs for water.

THE PLANTS OF AUSTRALIA

Left: The desert eucalyptus survives dry conditions well.

Many different types of plants grow across Australia, depending on the temperature and amount of rainfall in each region. Some of these plants gave the Aboriginal people fruit, seeds, greens, flowers, herbs, and spices for food.

From Rain Forests to Desert Survivors

Tropical northern Australia is home to thick rain forests. Mangrove trees grow in the swamps. Australia also has many types of eucalyptus and acacia trees. Eucalyptus trees have fragrant green leaves and are valued for their wood and oil. Most acacia trees have clusters of yellow flowers. Australia's desert plants include baobab trees, cacti, grasses, and shrubs. The baobab is a huge tree that stores water in its fat trunk.

Right: The trunk of a baobab tree can be as wide as 30 feet (9 meters) across.

The Bush Tomato

The bush tomato was an important desert fruit for Aboriginal people. It looks like a small green tomato and grows on a low prickly shrub. In the heat of summer, bush tomatoes dry on the bush into sweet "raisins." Aboriginal people sometimes collected the dried tomatoes, ground them with water into a thick paste, and rolled the paste into balls. To help preserve them, people covered the balls with red ocher (a type of earth) and dried them in the sun. These large balls of fruit could be stored for several years.

Above: The bush tomato plant blooms with small pretty flowers.

Dangerous Ancient Plants

The cycad is an ancient kind of tree that first grew in the time of the dinosaurs. It looks like a palm tree. Cycads grow in tropical northern Australia. They produce large cones full of seeds, but without special preparation the seeds are poisonous. The crew of the *Endeavour*, the first English ship to reach Australia, became very ill after eating the seeds. Aboriginal women knew how to remove the poison by placing the seeds in bags under running water for several days. Seeds that had been soaked in water for several months or exposed to the sun, wind, and rain for a long time on the ground were also safe to eat. When the poison was gone, the women ground the seeds into flour and baked it over coals to make a kind of bread. Some modern Aboriginal women know how to make cycad seeds safe to eat.

QUANDONGS

The quandong is a well-known outback tree. Its bright red fruit (*right*) is a favorite food of emus. The fruit contains large knobbly seeds. Early European settlers in Australia used these seeds to make jewelry, buttons, and playing pieces for games. The fruit is rich in vitamin C, and the seeds are rich in oil and protein. The quandong is a parasitic plant—it attaches itself to the roots of other plants and draws nutrients from them. Some modern Australians grow quandongs on farms.

AUSTRALIA'S ANCIENT PEOPLE

Aboriginal people believe that their ancestors were created at the beginning of the world and that the Aboriginal people have always lived in Australia. Scientists think that the ancestors of the Aboriginal people might have come from parts of Asia or Africa. They arrived in Australia at least 40,000 years ago, maybe even more than 100,000 years ago. They probably traveled in boats and rafts and walked across pieces of land that once bridged the continents. The sea has since covered these land bridges.

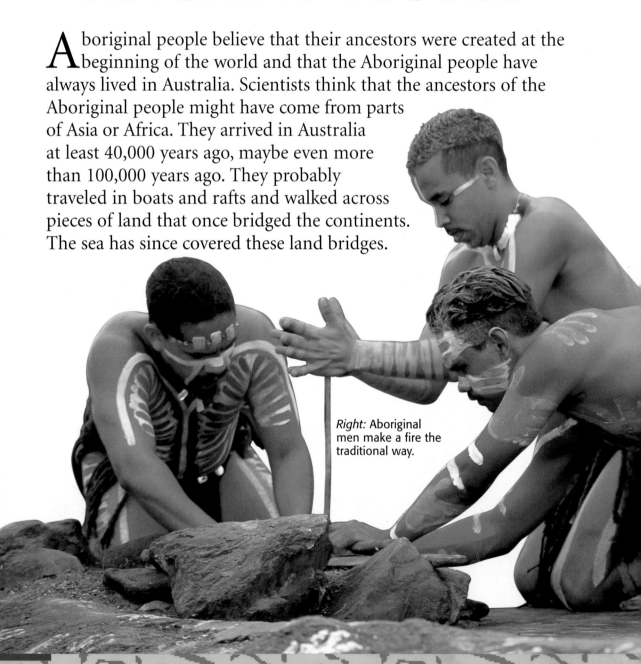

Right: Aboriginal men make a fire the traditional way.

Ancient Homelands

Aboriginal people once lived throughout Australia. They were divided into at least 250 groups with a common religion but different customs and languages. Smaller groups made up of one or several families (about six to forty people) lived and traveled together.

People's lifestyle varied a great deal, depending on where they lived. Desert groups moved often, over a wide area, in search of water and food. Groups in wetter areas stayed in a fairly small region, moving just two or three times a year. Each group occupied a certain homeland and respected the homelands of others. Groups needed permission to travel through someone else's land.

Above: Torres Strait Islanders were living on Murray Island long before Europeans arrived.

Hunting and Gathering

To obtain food, Aboriginal men hunted large animals like kangaroos and emus and caught sea cows, turtles, and seals in the sea. Women caught smaller animals, such as lizards, snakes, and possums. Aboriginal people also dug up roots and gathered fruit, seeds, and eggs for food. Aboriginal people made many kinds of tools: knives, spears, axes, and shields. They made awls (pointed tools used to make holes in animal skins or wood) from echidna spines and other kinds of animal bones. They also made containers, including water bags, baskets, and large bowls.

MAKING FIRE

Aboriginal people used fire to provide warmth, keep insects away, cook and dry food, harden and sharpen tools, and smoke animals out of hollow logs or drive them toward hunters. Aboriginal people made fire by rubbing together pieces of wood or hard rocks to produce heat and then sparks.

EUROPEAN INVADERS

Before the late 1700s, Indonesian merchant ships visited Australia, looking for supplies and food items to trade. In the 1700s and 1800s, European ships arrived. In 1770, English captain James Cook sailed along the eastern coast of Australia in his ship the *Endeavour*. The ship landed at Botany Bay, the site of present-day Sydney. Eighteen years later, Captain Arthur Phillip arrived with hundreds of English convicts. English prisons were full, and faraway Australia seemed like a good place to send the lawbreakers. These convicts were some of the first Australian settlers. After serving their prison sentences, they set up farms and towns. Other Europeans came to Australia of their own free will.

Culture Clash

Most Europeans looked down on the Aboriginal people because they didn't have farms, clothes, or books like the Europeans did. In turn, the Aboriginal people couldn't understand the foreigners' practices. In Aboriginal culture, everything, including tools and food, was shared. So Aboriginal people sometimes took the newcomers' belongings. This angered the Europeans.

More Conflicts

White settlers built fences around their homes and farms and drove the Aboriginal people off their traditional lands. Some Europeans poisoned and shot Aboriginal people. Aboriginal weapons, such as spears and sticks, did little to harm the enemy. With horses and guns, the Europeans defeated the Aboriginal people in many clashes. In just over fifty years, the Aboriginal population of Botany Bay fell from 3,000 to only 300.

The newcomers brought diseases from Europe. Because the Aboriginal people had never suffered from these diseases before, they had no built-in protection against them. Thousands died from smallpox, measles, influenza, and other illnesses.

The foreigners also brought alcohol, a substance that Aboriginal people had never known before. Many Aboriginal people became addicted to alcohol, a problem that remains in many Aboriginal communities.

Left: When they came to Australia in the 1700s and 1800s, European explorers met Aboriginal groups.

EYRE AND WYLIE

In 1841, Englishmen Edward John Eyre (*right*) and John Baxter left Adelaide on a journey to explore Australia's barren southern coast, along the Great Australian Bight. They took with them three Aboriginal men, one named Wylie. The Englishmen wanted food carefully rationed—using only what was necessary and saving extra supplies for the future. But the Aboriginal men were used to eating whenever food was plentiful and hunting game when it was available. The other two Aboriginal men shot Baxter and ran away with the supplies, leaving Wylie and Eyre. As they traveled through dry desert country, both men became very weak. But Wylie's skill at finding food and freshwater in the bush kept them both alive. When they reached Albany safely, Wylie became a hero.

DRIVEN OFF THE LAND

Between 1829 and 1901, English settlers set up states and governments across Australia. They made laws and expected the Aboriginal people to obey these laws.

The Killing Time

In 1928, in the Coniston Station area of the Northern Territory, an Aboriginal man killed a white man who had stolen his wife. White police officers responded by killing many Aboriginal people. The Coniston Massacre is only one of many such killings that began in the 1780s and continued well into the 1900s. Aboriginal people call this period "the killing time." White leaders rarely arrested or punished white people who committed the crimes.

The Role of the Church

From the 1830s onward, Christian churches grew in size and number across Australia. Missionaries (religious teachers) tried to explain Christianity to Australia's first people. The missionaries sometimes took Aboriginal children to religious schools, far away from their families.

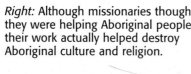

Right: Although missionaries thought they were helping Aboriginal people, their work actually helped destroy Aboriginal culture and religion.

The Stolen Generation

In the early 1900s, the Australian government tried to absorb Aboriginal people into European culture. The children of mixed Aboriginal and European marriages had light skin. The government wanted these children especially to give up their Aboriginal culture. From 1910 to 1970, officials took thousands of mixed-race children from their families and placed them

Above: Aboriginal girls in a church-run home in the 1950s

with white families or in church-run homes. Aboriginal people call this group "the stolen generation." Aboriginal mothers tried to hide their mixed-race children or to darken their skin with charcoal. Lots of the children never saw their families again. Many suffered beatings and other abuse at the hands of their white caretakers. As adults, they often became ill or depressed. Poor record keeping makes it impossible to know the exact numbers of stolen children.

LOWITJA O'DONOGHUE

Lowitja (Lois) O'Donoghue (*right*) was born in 1932 to an Aboriginal mother and an Irish immigrant father. When she was two years old, she was taken with her two sisters to a church-run home. There she was not allowed to speak her mother's language. When she grew up, she wanted to become a nurse. But in those days no hospital would hire Aboriginal nurses. So O'Donoghue helped organize public meetings to challenge the system. In 1954, she became one of the first Aboriginal nurse trainees at the Royal Adelaide Hospital. From 1990 to 1992, she served as the first chairperson of the Aboriginal and Torres Strait Islander Commission, an organization that defends the rights of Australia's first people.

FIGHTING FOR EQUALITY

Above: Some Aboriginal people worked for whites as station hands.

Beginning with the years of white settlement, many Aboriginal people were forced to live on special pieces of land called reserves, run by churches or the government. The reserves were often far away from traditional lands, and families could be split up. Rules were strict. People could not travel off the reserves freely, practice their old traditions, or speak their native languages.

Treated Differently

Aboriginal people were not allowed to mix with European people unless they carried special certificates stating that they had given up their Aboriginal identities. Few Aboriginal people could obtain an education or run their own businesses. Instead, Aboriginal people mainly worked for whites as station and farmhands, road and railway workers, and household help. Many restaurants and clubs refused to allow Aboriginal people inside.

Right: In the late 1900s, many Aboriginal people spoke out against unfair treatment from whites.

Early Protests

In the 1900s, the Aboriginal people started to fight for equal treatment. They demanded changes to Australia's constitution. The constitution did not recognize Aboriginal people as ordinary Australian citizens. It allowed the states to make laws for Aboriginal people. Some of these state laws were very unfair. The constitution also excluded Aboriginal people from the national census (population count). In 1965, thirty Sydney University students, led by Aboriginal man Charlie Perkins, took a 2,000-mile (3,220-kilometer) bus ride to investigate and protest racial discrimination. The group called themselves the Freedom Riders.

Above: The Freedom Riders in 1965

The 1967 Referendum

The political activity led to a referendum (a public vote) on May 27, 1967. More than 90 percent of Australians voted to remove the unjust sections of their constitution. The Australian government obtained the power to stop unfair state laws. For the first time, Aboriginal people were included in the national census and were officially part of Australian society. Many Aboriginal and white people welcomed the changes.

NEW FLAGS

In 1971, Aboriginal artist Harold Thomas designed a special flag (*above*) for the Aboriginal people. The color black on the flag stands for the people, red represents the land, and the yellow circle stands for the sun, which gives life. Bernard Namok, a fifteen-year-old student from Thursday Island, designed the Torres Strait Islander flag. This flag has two green bands that represent the land, a wide blue band that stands for the sea, and two black bands to represent the people. In the center is the *dhari*, the traditional Torres Strait Islander headdress. The five-pointed star represents the five island groups in the strait.

RESTORING FRIENDSHIP

In the late 1900s, the Australian government worked for integration. The government wanted Aboriginal people to live and work freely among whites. Many Aboriginal families moved away from reserves and into big cities. But the move was so sudden that some people could not cope in the different environment. Many struggled with poverty and other social problems, even after integration. To fight these problems, some Aboriginal people helped others create community groups, child-care centers, and legal and medical service centers. From 1980 to 1990, the Aboriginal Development Commission helped Aboriginal people buy or rent land, set up businesses, and obtain new houses.

Toward Understanding

In 1991, the Australian government established the Council for Aboriginal Reconciliation to encourage friendship between Aboriginal and non-Aboriginal Australians. In the 1990s, all the major church groups in the country apologized to Aboriginal people for adding to their pain and hardship.

Right: Aboriginal and white children mix freely, but many Aboriginal people still remember the injustices of the past.

Saying Sorry

Many Australians observed a national Sorry Day on May 26, 1998. On this day, white Australians signed hundreds of "sorry books" and presented them to Aboriginal leaders. Two years later, in May 2000, tens of thousands of Australians walked across city bridges as a show of apology.

The Right to the Land

Although Australia's first people had been living in the country for more than 40,000 years, the first Europeans in Australia believed in the idea of *terra nullius,* or "no one's land." They argued that nobody owned Australia's land and that it was theirs for the taking. The Europeans took the land by force, built farms and towns there, and made the Aboriginal people move to reserves. Since the 1970s, the Australian government has given some lands back to Aboriginal people, but there is still work to be done. Aboriginal people want to preserve their ancient sacred sites and teach non-Aboriginal people about traditional ways of caring for the land. They also want to protect the natural environment, including native plants and animals.

Above: Many Australians walked across Sydney Harbour Bridge on May 28, 2000, as a sign of apology to the Aboriginal people.

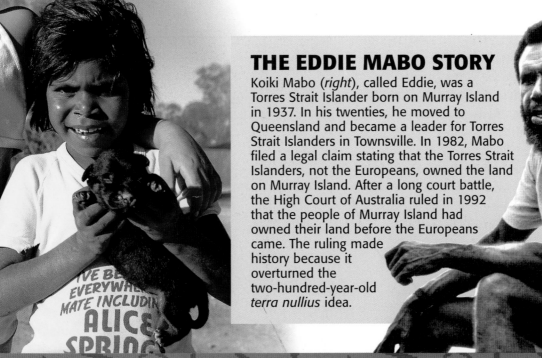

THE EDDIE MABO STORY

Koiki Mabo (*right*), called Eddie, was a Torres Strait Islander born on Murray Island in 1937. In his twenties, he moved to Queensland and became a leader for Torres Strait Islanders in Townsville. In 1982, Mabo filed a legal claim stating that the Torres Strait Islanders, not the Europeans, owned the land on Murray Island. After a long court battle, the High Court of Australia ruled in 1992 that the people of Murray Island had owned their land before the Europeans came. The ruling made history because it overturned the two-hundred-year-old *terra nullius* idea.

LIVING OFF THE LAND

Land was the basis of the Aboriginal economy. It provided not only food but also items for trade and sharing. Everybody in Aboriginal society helped one another. People who had plenty of food shared it with those who had little. Meat hunters shared with seed and berry gatherers so that everyone had a healthy, balanced diet. Those who were good at hunting, toolmaking, and the use of medicines taught others their skills. The older people could not do much physical work, but they taught others about sacred traditions and ceremonies.

A Trading People

By trading with one another, Aboriginal people could obtain goods that were not available in their own areas. The Torres Strait Islanders traded canoes, spears, drums, shells, feathers, and fruit. Aboriginal people in mainland Australia traded ocher, weapons, shells, plants, containers, and animal-skin cloaks. People often carried trade items hundreds of miles and passed them from one group to the next. Some trade routes crossed Australia for thousands of miles.

Right: For Aboriginal people, food traditionally came from the land.

The Right to Hunt and Gather

Aboriginal people generally did not trade food because most foods spoiled over long journeys. However, the right to the food in a certain area was used in trading. For instance, the Ngarigo and Djilamatang people lived in the Snowy Mountains of southeastern Australia, where millions of edible bogong moths hatched in late spring. The local people could not preserve extra moths for eating later, so they welcomed neighboring groups to come share the feast. When food in the mountains became scarce, these same neighbors allowed the Ngarigo and Djilamatang onto their lands to hunt and gather food.

Above: An ocher mine in South Australia

Trading for Ocher

Ocher is a kind of earth that ranges in color from light yellow to brown or red. Aboriginal people used ocher for rock painting and to decorate their bodies for ceremonies. Shiny, high-quality ocher was very valuable. People from far away came to the Flinders Ranges in South Australia to trade tools and plants for ocher dust. To enter the ocher mines, outsiders had to get permission from the Adnyamathanha elders, the caretakers of the mines. Otherwise, the elders would attack the outsiders.

PITURI

Some Aboriginal people liked to chew and smoke the dried leaves of the pituri plant. The best pituri grew in Queensland. Pituri was valuable for trading. Aboriginal people carefully guarded their knowledge of the plant. Only certain men were allowed to harvest it. Traders carried pituri more than 900 miles (1,448 kilometers), from the Gulf of Carpentaria in the north to Spencer Gulf in the south.

23

THE MODERN ECONOMY

Modern Aboriginal people have a great variety of lifestyles and jobs. Some make their living in traditional ways, such as by painting or toolmaking. Other Aboriginal people work in modern business. They work as factory workers, mechanics, shop clerks, teachers, nurses, lawyers, and politicians.

Money from Tourism

Many Aboriginal people work in the tourist industry. Anangu Tours is an Aboriginal-owned tour company that operates in Uluru-Kata Tjuta National Park, in the Northern Territory. Anangu tour guides tell visitors age-old stories about how their ancestors believed the world was created. The guides also demonstrate ancient bush survival skills. They speak in their traditional language, and interpreters translate their words into English.

Above: Aboriginal arts and crafts are popular souvenirs.

Mining on Aboriginal Lands

Australia is rich in minerals, including iron ore, aluminum, coal, silver, and gold. Many minerals are located on Aboriginal lands. Aboriginal people often allow companies to mine on their land, as long as the companies agree to protect the land and their culture and to make payments to the people who live there. Companies must also agree not to destroy or remove rocks from sacred sites.

Artifacts for Sale

Many Aboriginal artists make traditional objects to sell and use. These objects include baskets, bags, and large wooden bowls; musical instruments, tools, and weapons; and decorations such as carved animals. Aboriginal artists also make nontraditional craft items, such as pottery, leatherwork, jewelry, carved emu eggs, and glasswork. These are sold in Aboriginal cultural centers and in craft shops throughout Australia and the world.

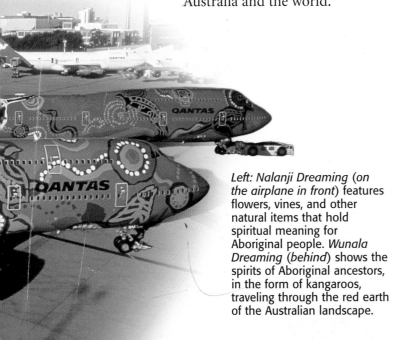

Left: Nalanji Dreaming (on the airplane in front) features flowers, vines, and other natural items that hold spiritual meaning for Aboriginal people. *Wunala Dreaming (behind)* shows the spirits of Aboriginal ancestors, in the form of kangaroos, traveling through the red earth of the Australian landscape.

A BUSINESS SUCCESS STORY

Taken from his family in the Northern Territory when he was five years old, John Moriarty grew up thousands of miles from his homeland. In the 1960s, he became the first Aboriginal college student in South Australia. In 1983, Moriarty and his wife, Ros, set up a successful design firm called Jumbana (John's Aboriginal name). In the mid-1990s, the company created two paintings for Qantas Airways. The pictures, *Wunala Dreaming* and *Nalanji Dreaming*, were scanned into a computer, enlarged onto 1.2 miles (2 kilometers) of tracing paper, and then painted onto airplanes. Jumbana continues to make money by selling its many designs for clothing and accessories.

AT HOME ON THE LAND

To be near the animals they hunted and the plants and fruit they gathered, Aboriginal people built houses close to water sources, which the plants and animals needed for survival. Few of these homes were permanent. As food supplies decreased or water dried up, people moved in search of new supplies.

Above: Bark was treated with smoke, which hardened it. As a result, bark shelters could last up to a year or two.

Bark Shelters

Different groups built different kinds of houses across Australia. The Kuku-yalanji people of Queensland built large dome-shaped shelters with bark cut from living trees. The houses' frames were made of saplings (thin branches) bent into semicircles. People in other areas made bark houses with flat or peaked roofs.

Other Kinds of Houses

In Tasmania, the southern island state with the coldest winters in Australia, the Toogee people built large dome-shaped houses made of grass and other plant material and decorated with feathers. A bark lining provided protection from the weather, and the houses had room inside for a fire. In Victoria, archaeologists have found the remains of stone houses. These houses were U-shaped and open on one end, with walls about 3 feet (1 meter) high. The roofs were made from rushes and bark. The Nunggabuyu people of Arnhem Land in the Northern Territory still build houses that look like bark shelters, except the builders use modern materials such as iron and Masonite (a compact building material made from wood fiber).

Inside the Houses

The size of a bark house depended on the number of people who needed to live in it—usually between six and twenty-five. Family groups or groups of single men shared one house.

Aboriginal houses had no walls to divide rooms. But houses had special places for each different activity—to prepare food or for children to play, for example. In some houses, people built fire pits for cooking and warmth and to keep away insects.

Left: Most modern Aboriginal people live in modern-style houses made of wood, stone, and brick.

SPECIAL POSITIONS

The arrangement of houses in an Aboriginal settlement was important. For instance, in a large group, relatives built their homes close together. Young married men lived near their fathers, and single men lived separately from families. Many modern aborigines live in towns and cities. But as much as possible, especially in rural areas, they still prefer to position houses according to their relationships. This system shows order in the community.

THE TRADITIONAL LIFESTYLE

While Europeans often found the Australian climate harsh and the landscape uninviting, Aboriginal people felt thoroughly at home there. Aboriginal groups lived across the whole of Australia, even in the desert. They knew how to track and catch animals, what plants provided food and medicine, and how to make tools, nets, bags, containers, canoes, and houses from what the land provided.

Bugs Are Good to Eat!

Insects—ants, grubs, caterpillars, and moths—were an important source of food for many Aboriginal people. Along the coast, Aboriginal people ate long white worms cut from mangrove trees. In remote parts of Australia, some groups still eat insects.

Above: The witchetty grub is eaten raw or roasted over a fire.

Left: Spears were traditionally made from wood.

Spears for Hunting and Fishing

Some spears were simple poles without spearheads. Others had detachable heads. Harpoons (spears with ropes attached) were used for killing sea animals, such as sea cows, seals, and turtles. Fishing spears had two or three sharp points. Aboriginal people also used spears to hunt kangaroos, emus, and other animals.

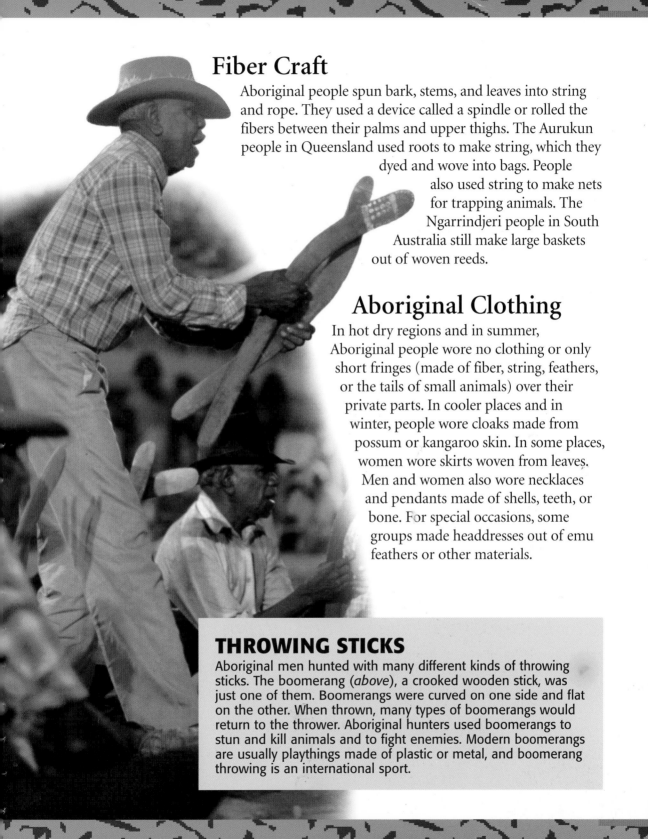

Fiber Craft

Aboriginal people spun bark, stems, and leaves into string and rope. They used a device called a spindle or rolled the fibers between their palms and upper thighs. The Aurukun people in Queensland used roots to make string, which they dyed and wove into bags. People also used string to make nets for trapping animals. The Ngarrindjeri people in South Australia still make large baskets out of woven reeds.

Aboriginal Clothing

In hot dry regions and in summer, Aboriginal people wore no clothing or only short fringes (made of fiber, string, feathers, or the tails of small animals) over their private parts. In cooler places and in winter, people wore cloaks made from possum or kangaroo skin. In some places, women wore skirts woven from leaves. Men and women also wore necklaces and pendants made of shells, teeth, or bone. For special occasions, some groups made headdresses out of emu feathers or other materials.

THROWING STICKS

Aboriginal men hunted with many different kinds of throwing sticks. The boomerang (*above*), a crooked wooden stick, was just one of them. Boomerangs were curved on one side and flat on the other. When thrown, many types of boomerangs would return to the thrower. Aboriginal hunters used boomerangs to stun and kill animals and to fight enemies. Modern boomerangs are usually playthings made of plastic or metal, and boomerang throwing is an international sport.

RELATING TO ONE ANOTHER

In traditional Aboriginal culture, community and family were very important. Everyone helped care for children and elderly people and shared work and responsibility. Strict kinship, or family, rules governed how people behaved toward one another.

Kinship Rules

Certain people in Aboriginal society were not supposed to have contact with each other. For example, a man and his mother-in-law had to avoid contact with each other and communicate only through a third person. Adult brothers and sisters had to face different directions when they talked to each other. In another kinship tradition, a woman called her mother's sisters "mother," and they called her "daughter." In this way, everyone had several "parents."

Right: Aboriginal children play together.

Rules about Marriage

Families arranged most marriages, and some children were promised in marriage even before they were born. Girls usually married in their early teens. In some groups, their husbands were many years older. Many modern Aboriginal marriages do not follow the traditional rules and customs.

Sending Smoke Signals

Aboriginal people communicated over long distances using smoke signals. Newly cut wood made dark smoke, while dry wood produced light-colored smoke. By blowing smoke or waving bark over the fire, people could make rising smoke take different shapes, such as columns, spirals, and puffs. The color and shape of the smoke carried different meanings. Smoke signals announced news, warned about visitors and enemies, or asked for help in carrying home animals from a hunt.

Above: Many present-day Aboriginal families combine their traditions with modern lifestyles.

Message Sticks

Aboriginal people also sent messages using wooden sticks that measured from 8 to 24 inches (20 to 61 centimeters) long. Some sticks were simple. Others were decorated with carving, paint, or feathers. Patterns on the sticks were something like reminders. For instance, three notches in a stick might mean that three elders were sending an invitation. The same stick could be used over again to carry a different message.

A POLITICAL MESSAGE

In 1974, the Aboriginal people of Mornington Island in the Gulf of Carpentaria sent three men with message sticks to the Australian prime minister and the premier of Queensland. The message sticks urged the officials to hurry up and settle a land rights dispute while the parties were still on friendly terms.

EDUCATION AND HEALTH CARE

When the Europeans arrived in Australia, they forced the Aboriginal people to give up their traditional systems of education and health care. In recent times, Aboriginal people have found ways to combine their traditional methods with modern schools and medical practices.

Below: An Aboriginal teacher shows his student how to throw a boomerang.

Two Systems of Education

Traditional Aboriginal education took place outdoors. Parents and older relatives taught children to hunt, fish, gather, make clothes, build houses, and trade. But from the 1800s to the 1970s, Aboriginal children had to attend European-style schools. There, teachers gave lessons in English and held classes indoors. Because the children no longer learned from their elders, a lot of traditional knowledge was lost.

Adapting to Modern Society

In recent years, many Aboriginal communities have set up schools that teach both traditional knowledge and modern subjects. The children go on field trips and camping trips to learn about their language and culture. Activities might include collecting bush food and medicine, fishing, and catching shellfish.

Traditional Health Care

In Aboriginal society, women knew which plants could cure common illnesses. They also performed ceremonies to maintain people's health. Healers, who were more like doctors, were mainly men. They treated the sick in various ways. Sometimes healers sang until patients got better. Sometimes they asked spirits for advice.

The Europeans came to Australia with outside diseases that killed many Aboriginal people. Forced off their traditional lands and away from healing plants and nutritious bush food, many Aboriginal people became sick. But in the 1960s, state governments began to provide Aboriginal people with medical care.

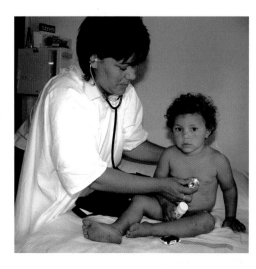

Above: A doctor examines an Aboriginal baby at a clinic.

Giving Birth the Traditional Way

In the past, Aboriginal women gave birth in the bush, with their mothers helping them. After Europeans arrived, Aboriginal women began to go to hospitals to give birth. Hospitals were safer and cleaner than the bush, but the women often felt alone, away from their people and customs. In some parts of Australia, Aboriginal women are returning to traditional customs. At the Alukura Birthing Centre in Alice Springs, for instance, traditional midwives (women who help mothers in childbirth) are part of the staff. They uphold Aboriginal women's law, which does not allow mothers to eat certain foods during pregnancy.

TEACHING THROUGH STORIES

Storytelling was an important teaching tool in Aboriginal culture. Traditional storytellers told their tales with full facial expressions and plenty of body movement. Through stories, the storytellers could entertain, advise, correct, guide, comfort, or say sorry to a listener.

PICTURES AND WORDS

The Aboriginal people believe that their ancestors created the world and live on as spirits. Through painting, storytelling, singing, dancing, and playing music, modern Aboriginal people can connect with their ancestors and keep the land and the spiritual world in harmony.

Painting

Aboriginal people painted designs on rock, bark, sacred objects, and the ground. They also painted their bodies. Traditional designs were made up of lines, dots, circles, and swirls that had different meanings to different groups. The designs often told stories or stood for natural features or forces and the spirits that created the world.

Rock art took many forms. Some artists pounded or chipped away layers of rock to reveal different colored rock beneath. Others mixed white clay, red or yellow ocher, or charcoal with water to make paint.

Left: Aboriginal people still practice many ancient arts, and many sell their artwork for a living.

Bark Art

In southern Australia, people used charcoal to make patterns on bark shelters. They also scratched designs into bark that had been blackened by fire. Some bark paintings from western Arnhem Land show the inner organs of animals, sort of like X-ray pictures. Other bark paintings were used to cover graves.

Above: An Aboriginal rock painting at Kakadu National Park, Northern Territory

Writing

The Aboriginal people traditionally did not have a written language, but many modern Aboriginal writers have gained fame. Kevin Gilbert, a Wiradjuri man, wrote *The Cherry Pickers,* the first English play written by an Aboriginal person. *We Are Going,* a book of poetry written by Oodgeroo Noonuccal in 1964, was the first book ever published by an Aboriginal person. Sally Morgan was born in Perth in 1951 to a white father and a part-Aboriginal mother. Her book *My Place* (1987) tells the story of how she discovered her Aboriginal ancestry. Morgan is also famous as an artist.

Above: Oodgeroo Noonuccal was a respected poet, writer, and artist. She worked for Aboriginal rights.

EVERYONE'S AN ARTIST!

Aboriginal people did not regard art as a special activity that only some people did. Painting (*left*), telling stories, playing music, and dancing were all part of their religious beliefs and part of normal everyday life. In that sense, every Aboriginal person was an artist.

MUSIC AND DANCE

Music and dance flow through every part of Aboriginal life. People believe that these art forms close the time gap between past and present. Music and dance also draw the singers and dancers into harmony with the spirits of their ancestors. Aboriginal music was originally used to help in birth and healing, comfort the grieving, and help the spirits of the dead depart. People also performed songs and ceremonies in exchange for goods. In modern times, Aboriginal music is used to teach lessons, tell stories, perform ceremonies, and record history.

Below: Singing and chanting accompany an Aboriginal dance.

Above: Aboriginal dancers perform with traditional musical instruments.

Songs and Dances

Aboriginal songs described and told the locations of land formations and water sources. Many modern Aboriginal people accurately sing the old songs, with little or no change in form, words, pitch, rhythm, or length. Other singers combine traditional songs and instruments with modern music.

In the past, Aboriginal people danced to tell stories and as part of rituals. Dancers often imitated the movements of animals, such as kangaroos and emus. Many modern dance companies have brought back the old dances. Dances might tell about ancient legends or about more recent events such as World War II. Some groups combine new dance styles with Aboriginal styles that date back thousands of years.

Musical Instruments

The main instrument of Aboriginal music is the human voice, but people use other instruments, too. They use clap sticks (two sticks rhythmically clapped together), including boomerangs. The rasp is a saw-toothed stick that produces musical sounds when rubbed across another stick. The Torres Strait Islanders make a drum from a long hollow piece of wood with snakeskin stretched across one end. People also clap hands, slap their thighs or buttocks, and make various kinds of voice calls to accompany singers. In recent years, modern musicians have added guitars and leaf whistles to traditional musical sounds.

THE DIDJERIDU

The *didjeridu* (*right*), a kind of trumpet or horn, was originally played in northwestern parts of Australia. The instrument is still popular among modern musicians. The typical didjeridu was 40 to 60 inches (102 to 152 centimeters) long. It was made from a piece of a bamboo or a tree trunk hollowed out by termites or fire. A mouthpiece was made from wax or resin. The didjeridu player blew into the mouthpiece, vibrating the lips and tapping the instrument rhythmically with one hand.

ANCIENT LANGUAGES

Before the 1800s, at least 250 native languages were spoken in Australia. After the Europeans arrived, many languages were forgotten. Only about thirty or forty of the traditional languages are still spoken fluently. Some people use the old languages and speak English as a second language. But most modern Aboriginal people speak mainly English. Many Aboriginal people want to revive and learn their traditional languages.

Missionaries and Language

Until the Europeans came, Aboriginal people had no written language as we know it. Instead, Aboriginal people recorded their languages in songs and stories. They learned songs word for word and passed them down accurately from generation to generation. The songs described parts of their culture, history, and the land where they lived. After the Europeans arrived, many languages were forgotten. But in some areas, missionaries and anthropologists (people who study human cultures) wrote down the traditional languages using their own alphabets. In modern times, people have begun to write books in the Aboriginal languages and to teach people to speak, read, and write them at special schools.

Right: Many modern Aboriginal children attend schools where they learn both English and their traditional languages.

Bilingual Education

In the Northern Territory, some children grow up speaking mostly their traditional language. For these children, English is a second language. In 1972, the state government started a program to teach these children in both their own language and English. The children learn a few words of English in their first year of school. By seventh grade, about 80 percent of their lessons are in English, but they still learn important basic concepts of math and spelling in their own language.

A Rich Vocabulary

Aboriginal languages have words for everything in the natural environment and for many different kinds of spears, boomerangs, and tools. In most Aboriginal languages, the word *you* varies, depending on the speaker's relationship to the listener. Here are some examples from the Alyawarr language of central Australia:

Word	Pronunciation	Meaning
mpwelanth	ehm-PULL-uhnth	You two (not related to me through my father)
mpwelak	ehm-PULL-uhk	You two (related to me through my father—for example, my uncle and my uncle's son)
mpwel	ehm-PULL	You two (related to me through my father and in the same generation—for example, the children of two brothers)

ABORIGINAL DREAMING

Aboriginal people believe that in the very beginning, the spirits of their ancestors created the world and everything in it. Aboriginal Dreaming has nothing to do with the dreams that occur while we sleep. Instead, a person's Dreaming refers to his or her spiritual connection to the very beginning of all things. For Aboriginal people, the Dreaming spirits from the beginning of time are still active in the modern world. Through dancing, painting, singing, and storytelling, people renew their relationship with the spirits and the land.

Dreaming Stories

Modern Aboriginal people tell Dreaming stories about the beginning—a time before there were living things, when the land was flat and dark. As the Dreaming spirits moved through the landscape, they made land formations and living creatures. The spirits had the power to change shape and sometimes took the form of stars, rain, wind, or animals. Other Dreaming stories tell about sacred places and objects that Aboriginal people must treat with respect.

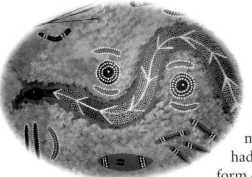

Above: Dreaming spirits are often painted in the form of animals.

Totems

Animals such as kangaroos and honey ants served as totems—special symbols assigned to Aboriginal families or individuals. Totems helped determine the relationships between people and groups. For instance, groups with totem animals that were enemies could not come into contact with each other.

Aboriginal Christians

European missionaries brought Christianity to Australia in the 1700s and 1800s. Some Aboriginal people converted to Christianity and combined their traditional beliefs with Christian beliefs. For instance, many modern Aboriginal Christians believe that the God in the Bible is also the traditional Great Spirit, the being who gave Aboriginal people their land and law.

Above: Traditional artwork decorates many Aboriginal Christian churches.

THREE SISTERS DREAMING

At the beginning of the world, seven Gundungurra sisters lived with their family at Katoomba near present-day Sydney. The sisters were giants. Three of them loved brothers from the neighboring Dharruk people, but ancestral law did not allow them to marry these men. The brothers attacked the Gundungurra people to claim the women by force. To protect the three sisters, the Clever Man took them to the top of a cliff and turned them into stone. He planned to return after the battle and change them back. But he was killed, and no one knew how to turn the three stones back into living women. The Gundungurra people believe that three rock formations (*left*) in their region are the stone sisters. The four other sisters went on to have children. That's why some modern Gundungurra women—descendants of the sisters—are very tall. The Clever Man still watches over the stone sisters. He is known as Witch's Falls.

THE LAWS OF THE ANCESTORS

Although the stories and ceremonies vary, all Aboriginal groups believe in the Dreaming. People also believe that the spirits of their ancestors laid down laws about how people should behave toward each other. Aboriginal children still learn about these laws.

Rights and Responsibilities

The land was very important in Aboriginal law. People respected the spirit forces in each place and obeyed the laws to keep order there. Dreaming laws also gave people rights to the land—the right to live in a certain place, survive on its resources, take care of it, and grant others the right to share or pass through it. Many Aboriginal people still believe in these traditional land laws.

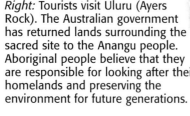

Right: Tourists visit Uluru (Ayers Rock). The Australian government has returned lands surrounding the sacred site to the Anangu people. Aboriginal people believe that they are responsible for looking after their homelands and preserving the environment for future generations.

Keeping the Law

In traditional Aboriginal communities, elders—both men and women—upheld the law. They settled disputes and punished lawbreakers. Going to forbidden places, mistreating certain relatives, fighting, or saying a dead person's name were all reasons for punishment. Penalties included verbal insults; wounding with a spear, knife, or club; or even death. As the next generation grew old enough, the elders passed on their knowledge of the law to them a little at a time.

Above: Aboriginal dancers perform before a sacred ceremony.

Reviving the Old Traditions

When European settlers put their own laws in place in the 1800s, the old Aboriginal laws were lost and no longer enforced. But some modern Australian authorities have started to respect Aboriginal law. In some cases, instead of punishing Aboriginal lawbreakers, judges send them back to their homelands to be dealt with by their elders.

THE RAINBOW SERPENT

Aboriginal law springs out of Dreaming stories, songs, and rituals. The law tells people how to behave. One of the most powerful ancestral beings is the Rainbow Serpent. As one of the first creators, the Rainbow Serpent taught the Aboriginal people their laws and ceremonies. Many people believe that disobeying these laws will make the serpent angry and bring floods, earthquakes, or other natural disasters.

FESTIVALS AND CEREMONIES

Aboriginal people performed ceremonies to show their respect for the spirits. Then everything on earth, such as the seasons and the growth of living things, would continue smoothly. Traditional ceremonies combined singing, dancing, body painting, and the wearing of special items, such as necklaces and headdresses.

Below: Aboriginal people of Cape York, Queensland, celebrate a festival.

Traditional Ceremonies

Whenever Aboriginal people gather to sing and dance, they are always celebrating their spiritual beliefs. In the past, gatherings were often very large, timed to take place when food was plentiful. People prepared by making special objects, getting the ceremony grounds ready, and painting their bodies. People often traded with one another and arranged marriages at public ceremonies. In modern times, many celebrations last for several days and involve whole communities. People build shelters for shade, paint their bodies, and make necklaces and headdresses while discussing stories. The most important parts of the celebrations are the songs and dances, especially those concerning land and home.

Above: Aboriginal people in Alice Springs perform a dance for tourists.

Funeral Traditions

Aboriginal people believe that when a person dies, his or her spirit stays close to familiar places. Traditionally, people burned a dead person's property and house to persuade the spirit to return to the spirit world. Sometimes, everyone in a settlement would move away after a person died, to persuade his or her spirit to leave. When someone dies in modern times, Aboriginal people do not burn his or her house or property. These would be costly to replace. Instead, people leave the house closed and empty. The remaining family members move in with relatives. When the community elders believe that the spirit has left the house, the family moves back in.

Left: Aboriginal men at a funeral

ALL KINDS OF HEADDRESSES

Headdresses vary throughout Australia, from simple headbands and feathers to elaborately cut and colored hairdos. Designs are related to Dreamings, and all the dancers in a performance usually wear the same style. During their dances, Torres Strait Islanders wear a large and elaborate headdress called the dhari.

GLOSSARY

aborigine: one of the original or earliest known inhabitants of a country or place

anthropologist: a scientist who studies human cultures

archaeologist: a scientist who studies the remains of past human cultures

discrimination: unfair and unjust treatment of a group of people, often based on race or another cultural difference

fossil: the remains of a plant or animal that lived thousands or millions of years ago

integration: the bringing together of different cultural groups into society on equal footing

interpreter: someone who translates a conversation between people who speak different languages

kinship: involving a family relationship

marsupial: a mammal group in which the females nurse their young in pouches

missionary: a religious teacher who sets out to convert others to his or her faith

parasitic: relying on another plant or animal for nutrition and survival

rationed: distributed day by day in portions

referendum: a vote by the public

terra nullius: no one's land; the idea that no one owned the land in Australia before the Europeans arrived in the 1700s

tor: a giant rock or hill

totem: an animal or object adopted as the symbol of a group or individual

FINDING OUT MORE

Books

Darlington, Robert. *Australia. Nations of the World* series. Austin, Texas: Raintree Steck-Vaughn, 2000.

Finley, Carol. *Aboriginal Art of Australia: Exploring Cultural Traditions. Art Around the World* series. Minneapolis: Lerner Publications Company, 1999.

North, Peter. *Australia. Countries of the World* series. Milwaukee, Wisconsin: Gareth Stevens, 1998.

Sutton, Peter, Christopher Anderson, and Philip Jones. *Dreamings: The Art of Aboriginal Australia.* New York. George Braziller, 1997.

Videos

Dreamtime of the Aborigines. A&E Home Video, 2000.

National Geographic's Australia's Aborigines. National Geographic, 1997.

Websites

<http://cf.vicnet.net.au/aboriginal/>

<http://www.aboriginalaustralia.com/>

<http://www.dreamtime.net.au/main.cfm>

<http://www.ea.gov.au/heritage/>

Organizations

Aboriginal and Torres Strait Islander Commission
P.O. Box 17
Woden ACT 2606
Australia
Tel: (61) 2 6121 4000
Website: <http://www.atsic.gov.au>

The Australian Institute of Aboriginal and Torres Strait Islander Studies (AIATSIS)
G.P.O. Box 553
Canberra, ACT 2601
Australia
Tel: (61) 2 6246 1111
Fax: (61) 2 6249 7310
Website: <http://www.aiatsis.gov.au/>

The Foundation for Aboriginal and Islander Research Action (FAIRA)
Box 8402 Woolloongabba Q 4102
Australia
Tel: (61) 7 3391 4677
Fax: (61) 7 3391 4551
E-mail: <letterbox@faira.org.au>
Website: <http://www.faira.org.au>

INDEX

ABOUT THE AUTHOR

Anne Bartlett is a non-Aboriginal freelance writer living in Adelaide, South Australia. She writes fiction and nonfiction for adults and children, and serves the Aboriginal community as a collaborative writer. She is currently working on two life story projects funded by the Division of State Aboriginal Affairs. She would like to thank all Aboriginal readers for their valuable feedback. Thanks also go to the Gundungurra women for permission to publish the story of the Three Sisters.

PICTURE CREDITS

(B=bottom; C=center; I=inset; L=left; M=main; R=right; T=top)

Ali Murat Atay: 23T • ANA Press Agency 44–45M • Archive Photos/Hulton Getty Picture Library: 13T, 15R, 16–17M, 17T • Brian Walters: 11T, 11B • Christine Osborne Pictures: 2, 26T, 33T, 34B, 41T, 45R • Dave G. Houser: 25T • Didier Noirot: 22–23M • Focus Team—Italy: 36–37 • G. Deichmann/ANA Press Agency: 18T, 28–29M, 35B • Haga Library: 3B, 37B, 46 • HBL: 18–19M, 30, 31 • The Hutchison Library: cover, 38–39M • International Photobank: 10L • Kay Shaw Photography: 9R, 34–35M, 41C • Liba Taylor: 6–7M, 42–43M • NewsPix: 17B, 19T, 21B, 21T, 32–33M, 35C, 39T • Oliver Bolch: 7T, 8L, 8–9M, 28BL, 40–41M • Photobank Photolibrary: 10–11M, 48 • Qantas Airways: 24–25M • Topham Picturepoint: 20–21M • Travel Ink/Jeff Goodman: 12–13M, 36 • Travel Ink/Jeremy Philips: 6C • Trip Photographic Library: title page, 4, 14–15M, 26–27M, 28C, 44L, 47 • Zafer Kizilkaya: 43T